ARE YOU A KID?

CHARLES PLYMELL

CHERRY VALLEY EDITIONS

(c) copyright 1977 by Charles Plymell
All rights reserved.
First edition.

Some of these poems have appeared in various magazines.

Library of Congress Cataloging in Publication Data
Plymell, Charles
   Are you a kid?

   I. Title.
PS3566.L95A9   811'.5'4   77-12698
ISBN 0-916156-28-1 signed
ISBN 0-916156-25-7 pbk.

Typesetting by Ed Hogan/Aspect Composition,
66 Rogers Ave., Somerville, Mass. 02144

Printed in the United States of America

"to all the kids in school"

POET'S PREFACE

For the most part these poems were written in the past few years while working in elementary and high schools in the eastern states.

The exposure to the sheer energy and force of youthful inquisitiveness was quite enough for a renewal of the flame in the fires of my own life as well as a source of inspiration.

One instance that took place in the far reaches of rural Pennsylvania is still vivid in my "mind's eye" and I'm sure I touched heads with the muse that day. The title of my book comes from that instance when an anonymous playmate asked, "Are you a kid?" I dedicate it "to all the kids in school" to make sure she is included.

It was a cool crisp day with the sun shining brightly. The children were bundled up for recess. Two boys were busy rolling around picking up the freshly cut grass and razing the piles constructed by the girls. They ate the grass, mocking the cows, and put some atop my head. I began to roll in the grass too. After a long studied look with the sun accentuating the pure space, the little girl asked, "Are you a kid?" The overwhelming imagination as moments of poetry flash by while children hug and tug for more is quite overwhelming at times.

The middle schools, or intermediate, or junior high students seem to have a continuous blitz of spontaneity. They all seem a bit Dada and more than once I've introduced this particular school of poetry to them, or at least the poetry of Gertrude Stein or Vachel Lindsay in which they seem to have a lot of fun with the abstract repititions. I think that at that age they prefer, perhaps unconsciously, a more rote or repeated exercise. (A good method to maintain calm in the rollicking seas of adolescence.) In high schools most students are typically impatient, bored, wary of strangers, super-sensitive, highly emotional and *very inexperienced.* They prefer softer nature poetry or love poetry, rather than the intellectual or harsher tones of a Pound or Eliot. Since they are all too eager to write very little on very limited experiences, I devised my own methods of having them fill pages with a new world of images before making the poem. The notion that language can be used for something other than daily conversations or filling out forms is a new concept to many of them. They have grown up with other forms of communication easily accessible. The direction seemed toward a non-verbal generation.

Once a trust is established though, there seems to be a real desire and effort to learn something from a stranger or outsider. They love honesty. And as soon as they see that something can be made from living language as one would make a painting or tapestry, they begin to invest their efforts.

It is certainly beneficial for me as a poet to be exposed to these "seasons of life" and to keep regenerating all the vast currents of poetry. Silly, Dada, imaginative, honest, sensitive, innocent. It's all there, and the freshness of the youthful vision might indicate there is something too readily forgotten in our day to day efforts toward a better future. The young have an interest in this, both biological and philosophical. It never hurts to listen to them. I like to. In fact I have to ask myself the same question at times: "Are you a kid?"

Charles Plymell

ARE YOU A KID?

THE SCHOOLHOUSE

Like a kid
I roll
in the fresh cut grass
build hills of it
toss it in the air
throw it on the hair
of bad boys
who try to kick open
the horizon,
to bring fresh dreams to class
where noses run, cheeks of sun
and thoughts
close the door behind them.

CALIFORNIA ORANGES

In nineteen and thirty-nine
you smelled the fragrance
of the orange groves
in California
you fainted from the freshness
of the sparkling water
down the washes
saw colors from Uncle Wiggly's garden

Before the honeycombed pattern
of chemical bees
flew into the migraine
we tried to kiss like

BIOGRAPHICAL DATA

I grew up
on thousands of acres.
Made miles of tunnels
through hideouts and forts.

But now I'm content
to grow
on two acres
where each movement is
a lifetime of gnats.

I know there is something
of everything in everything
very near us if we care to look.

But it could be said the "venturesome"
have gardened in delights of commerce;
knew such distances it made them wary.

The cat has the courage to enjoy itself.

FOR CYNARA

Once the poet goes behind the shades
once he draws the curtains
once the curtain of life is torn
once the certainty that eats
away the hours of the wall
and the wallpaper torn
to the pattern of the times.
Each pattern torn away or
stained to suit one's fancy
the impression of a day
the near-tide of your face
the memory washes back
into my eyes.
The Child near the tide
the innocence of hours wind.
My memory of you has been long
while I am lost in continuous repair.

SONG FRAGMENTS

Some people have their daily prayers,
Some have their daily affairs
But I just have my daily repairs.

Though I have been known to deal a little language
which has, I guess, a law of its own.
I never thought of myself as a sower
As in the fields are sown.

CHERRY VALLEY 1974

>When the day came back to me
>   I loved it
>   Elizabeth

Hot star over the river
The ring shaped like hydrogen
Over the line of sight
The window but a wavelength
And the light around the night

The village blends when lights go on
Into the sunset the hand connects
A game for winter nights from point to point

When icicles sprang in remote rotation
From the spring tooth harrow set some winters
Plow gear worn their own alignment
Walking John came over the hill
Ed the hermit honks past

And over sleepy hollow way moon
Lay super-highways monolithic ribbon
A ton of gravity under poured stone
Where workers leaned to structured plan
Engineers saw nerves in their own bindings
Some future civilization will observe

And I sleep like old Rip Van
With the bowling alley across the street

YOU FILL IN THE BLANKS

I got way down blue inside
that day,
drove west out of Albany...
toward a stretch of valleys
and high hills.

Like in the western states
that scarred their sunsets in me
many times before,
bottle at my feet,
red dirt canyon rim.

Back home the cold mountain hangs still,
I slip into my longjohns,
put on my earphones
lay back in a foam rubber flight.

Put on a record of Hank Williams' blues
confessed to a tune I didn't want to hear.

And I didn't know
where the magnetized needle
would take the full moon
burning outside my window.
Maybe a slight reading of biorhythms
would produce a flight pattern
into that milkweed sleeve
the crimson sunset lined against the space where I
could not aim my gliding flocks of memory....

RED WING

I care nothing for your mysteries
your fads and diets,
I saw Freedom throw a fake fur coat
into the Rio Grande,
I tell the faucets on the sink not
to stare back at me.

This world,
you know,
is being wrapped in machinery
with more cable than our minds can conceive.

With more layers of metal
than our nation's proudest mountain,
more tons of plastic
than marble in the ground.

We need more diaries of invisible beings
who have mined memories...
not like the coal strips in Kentucky

But like the metal
they chip from mountains
and pan from streams
to weigh and make rings of.

THE BALL IN THE WATER

The crystal ball
in which our eyes
forage the stars out
of the water.

To tell a gypsy a dam
was built over that little
mining town in Calif.

And it was all our stage
for a few nights...I hope
everyone has
those few nights,
while the curtain opens wide.

Because the eyes will soon become
a wreckage of nicotine and medication
and look like hardened milk.

But I remember the crystal air
in the mountains...
The wildflowers breeding,

I could graze
beneath the moon.

I could be a pony
and look wild at you.

THE HOCKEY PLAYER

goalie
with agility
like a hinged
flap hummingbird
eyes quick out of
armor skull fastest
ice split second point
the whole team in his hand
the long-haired falcon glide
beyond the hot blood of the pack
then slides as calm as dust settling
but fast and smooth like painless snow
the quick stick powdered sharp as skate
runners ruffles the neck held high among
the scissored mind of conquerors and warriors
of ice teeth crashes and cold spills and hot
blood players slide as fast as any puck across ice

WILMINGTON SKYLINE

Walking at night
under the unnatural green light
from a lamppost in Delaware,
I see the tower building windows
compute an image on a punch card
handled by an office worker at day.
A starling perches
on an intersection
not made of clay, but smooth cement
where potato chips become its prey.

The tribal surge begins and bones are picked
clean to resemble modish jewels
catching the light green
like eyes of rats
generating in worn garbage piles.

SUBWAY

> for Guy Waid

In confined space
unlit tubes
descend the vertigoes
behind the eyes

While wavey thought trains
of someone's days,
or hours, or histories
speed up to their eyes
and exit like a blur
of a blue graffiti engine.

The lusty chewing gum of Sunday
clacking like the sound of rails;

An ad from back of magazines
pops to life, standing in the aisle.
Familiar fireflies in unison.

I can very easily go insane
on the D train.

BOWERY BUMS

I see their tattered faces changing in the flame
above the barrel fires burning on the Bowery.

The torment of their souls paints pictures strange.
Their poetry pressed in the pavement resembling coins.

Their song the wailing sirens of the night,
Their hearts burned out in barrel fires
where big trucks beat the pavement day and night.

They hasten in the evening to unknown destinations:
old truckmen
raging in their rags, robes and hats
from mother's mystic closet.

They roam the streets like orators
making ragged gestures in the wind.

Julius Caesar,
Hamlet,
Robin Hood!

WHEN I LISTEN TO VERDI
for Jack Horton

I very rarely listen to Verdi
    but when I do hear Verdi
I know the ball is being shoved
    a little farther up the hill.

I don't care if my car's broke down
    when I listen to Verdi
I don't care how many times
    I see the tiger leap thru fire.

I don't care about the miles I drive
    on the interstate line
I don't care how hollow the cinder blocks seem
    when I listen to Verdi
waving the earth of dark green.

SURREALIZATION OF DREAMS

I'm afraid of such progress
and the urge to speak against the rust is gone.

I'm afraid of science
afraid to point my head north
that the one-sided guinea pig will die.

I'm afraid of the streets at night
that a landslide of barking grease will
chase me past the carbon copy of the blue light.

I've seen the ads flash past subway windows
and parts of aircraft jettison in space
I take them to bed with me
put them beneath the covers
and release them one by one.

THE PARK

The candy was warm
and the sun touched down
on the official park bench.
The wings of statues beat furiously!
And tons of copper and steel
came loose and went buoyant!
The people were really amazed.
They really got out there
and supported the event.

COASTLINE CLARITY

Poetry in my dinner plate
and poetry on the wall
I am writing poetry
for my big readings this fall.

I don't write any more good poems
I write bad ones to get well known.

Yes. I want to write new poems
clean as a whistle
on a mirror full of skates
that you can hear sometimes
flying around in the coastline of cities.

CUP OF JOE

Do you know
Truck Stop Joe
Dropped his load
In K.C.M.O.

Oh Oh
Truck Stop Joe
Longs for his boat
In Sausalito

Truck Stop Joe
Twitches across America
In the back of a truck
By the time he gets to Marin
He really wants to

Find a girl
Who wants to go

They just show him their bellies
And read the Tarot

PORTRAIT OF THE ART STUDENT
AS A GUILTY LIBERAL

She swings into the A&P
in a Volvo her folks bought for her,

her nose is turned up
and her face is spoiled,

the patches on her levis
are placed in just the right zone.

She is hard core creative
and has passed the labyrinth of beads.

Her giggles now labor over Ouspensky
and a quick course in Marxism one night.

The people in the long tired lines
of carefully selected food for soul

take special note of the food stamps
she takes from her purse so exactly.

TO A DEAD PIGEON:
UNDER THE FREEWAYS

Dead pigeon lying in the street
with your ingrown tongue so stringy,
I don't have to stop here and look at you
knowing I have to write a poem for you
and worst of all, only caring halfway
that you lie there in final arabesque.

You look like a bird pattern in a rug
only one dimension to the street,
an eagle you are, I've seen on Indian stone.
You no longer go with choo-choo neck
and spacemen eyes. You are beautiful there
beloved flyer who sought the crumbs of life.

But your form on the pavement will soon go away
first the feathers blue and grey,
your pinions crushed, your delicate ribs.
And you say, "who should want my feathers."
It's not the feathers but the flying...
you see. Caught in physics! astronomy!

Long thin muscles that once held the secrets
I want to give you ritual but I'm afraid,
afraid of walking past the blind with tin cups,
afraid there is not reason long enough—
to find my way home under the freeways.

IT'S FOR SURE ON A MOTORCYCLE

Blouse flowing in the wind
like a sky full of mirrors

Blowing through all barriers
of sink or thrill

Someone to hang onto
during cheap upheavals

in my mind
and to roll with
           somewhere

LISTENING TO CHARLEY CHRISTIAN
AND THINKING OF
HARLEM 1941

Yellow Buick convertible
on red brick road
loitering against the curb
sunny Sunday afternoon
Be Bop
cool live relaxed
Lucky Strike red wrapper
red apple
and ba-nan-a
back gold glaze
French Gypsy neon
Jam Jam Jam
tapestry session
Pennsylvania Hotel
Black La Salle!

NUEVA YORK
for Otis Redding

High above the iron bridge the sun peeks through
and all those broken hearts we painted on
were stuck upon the mainstays when the
horizon of graffiti overwhelmed the marshes.

I cannot climb the torch of plundering love
still burning, beckoning for touch.
Nor hit the stone crazy streets for money and life.
The door exposed the love-vine for years to come.

And I'm afraid of the spill of exchanges in Times Square
the untapped drama all night beyond the sub shops.
I do not know the dimensions of it all, and sometimes
forget the whispers out in the electric streets.

Things take on erotic proportions in the city
where each survivor makes a home next to death.
And not many take the time to look at the lesson
of the sunset where the super Falcon's eggs turn to dust.

Or imagine a hero inside the crystal ball while lights
turn orange and hip souls slip like clutches in dented cabs.
In the big night apple of the black sun the red lights
reflect in metal and Otis sings forever "Let me in."

NEW JERSEY COAST
AND THE STATUE OF LIBERTY

Fluorescent pebbles
thrown upon a phosphorescent beach
over lava of neon
spreading a new configuration
under orange and silver skies.
                        A chrome world
and a chrome sky
sealed chrome ball like Turner painted.
Those clouds where seagulls are a bright white
scare me like the ocean
coughing up bleached bones of poets lost in the sea
their minds chewed up.
The thought of where Crane might be
sends shivers through me.
Was he supposed to be protected by the green lady
standing in the sea with a poem at her feet
with her torch matched by the
torch of industry burning along the Pike.
Lights at sea
              too far away to be real,
many unanswerable things between
the shore and those lights.

BALTIMORE ECLIPSE

Did you see the sun blotted from the sky?
Like when the world ends and your hands
get cold and old women look witchy
and tell you strange tales. . . .
Did you see strangers arrive in a
field of straw and ice to warn
of the theft of the sun?
Who walks there with an idiot grin?
Who's that, and that, and that
who have no feathers nor shadows
when evening is two in the afternoon.
(Total over Virginia Beach and Edgar Cayce.)
I felt the ozone change. The cobalt door
creaks open. Noon was threatened.
Who may have crouched there, crouched there
before...unaware of cosmic superimposition.
Who was caught there, was caught there now
in the phantom's solid stare. Tell me this
is no sneak preview of things to come
lost in the garden of remembrance
where guards are stripped of their armor.
I saw the fairy tale stare painted on
doll's eyes of the wired man, flashing blue,
flashing blue, fixed on burning eels
swimming through the aether and grey
lads from Beatles movies in invisible aquarium.
But oh that sheen and dust of gold;
Oh that crisp acetylene evening,
the city awash with purple, and
birds folding their wings in afternoon.
The hour Poe arose from his statue
over there, and walked around.
I saw his musty hair fall to shoulder,
he stopped there to see his fellow
statues on the totem-slope of time
admiring their wings and horses.
Now down hill to reclaim his statue.
Over his shoulder, looking, looking.

MEMORIES OF 1403 GOUGH ST., S.F.

The back door and the tumbling grey stairs
where Neal returned "gone in the face" sd. Glen
where Betty and Frank slept off
cold alcohol nightmares. With T.V.
blaring Allen's poem about Kennedy written,
a slim thread of home to them all.

Maggie's wash from upstairs flapped viciously
where stranger histories blew
between the trees and dark lawns.

Awkward voices of birds flew from
the school in back—mortuary science.

I will never forget the clouds crashing
high above the jewelled ship of a city,
afloat like a suburban housewife's orange
peels insane among coffee grounds and bones.

Sailors of unrest, let the torch of amber
crawl upon the door between the lights,
and sleep upon that shady sea like clouds
floating into outports of eternity.

THE GARDEN DOOR AFAR

The interrogator came to the door
and asked who ate the golden ring

In a dark corner a crazed poet
wearing a brakeman's railroad cap
and green fluorescent lines down his pants
dreamed of lakes and geographical patterns
of heart attacks and impulses
between the daybreak of the stars
and the moon's last dark.

He will call me in his own voices
coming back through many people,
every day I will hear something
if it is only the wind
on the wheat or grass speaking.
I have been given a garden
of here and always.

THE TIME WE TIGHTENED THE BELTS

Packed up the mason jars and linen
"for the last time" as always.
Movin on again
because the tires slipped too
much in that snow and rain of time.
Because the belt that kept my
soul from slipping became threadbare
Like the face in a rainstorm that
never let up but lit up in lightning.

Like the tractor sinking in the pond
its laughing engine telling everyone it's drunk.

I'll order the necessary parts tomorrow
if I can find a way to town.

The truck is stuck and the
wheel fell off the Oliver,

the wrench I have won't fit
or I'd take the whole thing off,

and the company that makes 'em
is still on strike.

FOR STEVE

Down in Virginia
Where the green grass grows
Sings Jimmy Reed, who's not
been heard since instant mix.

I have driven the backroads
Where sleeping fences touched the sky,
Rode the interstate south of D.C.
over the battlefields with C.B. blaring.

Into the South which took me in its own time
I put the uniform of General Lee
over all our conversations.

STUDIO

I slept there until your
fragrance was gone
while my own masculinity
written in dust
began to settle again.

And the lights out the window
looked like a giant pinball machine.

The night was an ocean away.

I celebrate your necklace of armor and order
a profile of your royalty against the wall.
Perhaps you will see me in what I say
and send me a fish embroidered on a pillow
in the mail, one that can swim
through the window or the door.

DEEP DOWN

Freedom has thrown up on the bedsheet
the gainsy blue blanket
of Broadway's parkbench
The footprint on the moon
has since blown over
and the charm and the genes
won't play in the school yard.
And I can never get the corners of the sky
tucked around us sufficiently.

MAYDAY

I can distinguish the firey white teeth
and let the soot hide me,
overcome like feeling,
sensuous,
scary,
telepathic,
sound worth noting,
beaming on sunlight's white tilted dream...

The insomniac moth forced its way to the
twitter of my brain
and reminded me of the light left on
like a feeling inside your sweater
needed for the damp days of Spring...

THE BUGS OF AUGUST

You told me in a dream we all must die
That we have crawled into the plasma
Of the sun for an instant only

No sooner than we see the shape of life
Than the fear of opposites twists like roots
That blister in the body 'til
Lightning breathes and August swells

But I know the hot sidewalk where bugs
Of August, busy with self preparations,
Stop the walk of civilization,
Shunned by other passersby.

They will hear the vapor and light,
They talk and push and crawl until
The vacancy is full and the host
Will perish and be forgotten.

The old man I know will walk in
The village with his red cap
Pulled over his ears.
The hot sun wired to life
Shaped like skin
Around the shoulders.
All the bugs will busily detour.

SONNET

The Lord of Chance has loosed his planet beads,
As Thee alone, in vast decanter wane,
That time reveals a morning-glory seed
To sweet the hour of Thy daring pain.
No longer hopeless charter memory hold
The Tarot hand which spreads the stars array
But as flowers to adorning sun unfold;
The Sun loves Thee, as Thou the seed must play.
Though fear and hate have taken more than few,
As if their frames were pressed into a tomb,
We must with lips that kiss the morning dew
Sing like Nature, when in her private room.
    So subject caught King Self's dying net.
    At Nature's door we could at least be met.

SONNET

The rose that summer held—and gave again,
Has grown your form in re-appearing dew,
Preserved the fragrance of that time began
When seeds were drops of love in rose-red hue.
But sweet life must nourish on such sorrow,
As each dying makes some men blossom through
The blood that fell on each new tomorrow
And you saw this as I was watching you.
Under the influence of all your stars,
In mirrors of your galaxies of blue,
The hero and his love become your scars
But this rose picked could not be picked anew.
    To measure you and me in full disguise
    I lay beside our rose of paradise.

COWS

Looking in the face of cows
the way stockmen cruise beef cattle
the thing is
they don't care
cattle are queer
protein bulls on muscle beach
there was a *cow* magazine
with a cover of cows
hooked up to automatic milkers
if you drink milk before going
to bed you'll wake up with
a bovine face
cows are the milk of antiquity

DUSTY RIDE

I want a tattered shrine
around canvas slightly pale
designs all white in the white snow
I want to hold the madness on a crest of lilacs

when cherry trees are blown into
the cages of the mind
and love is in the last annex of space
I want to leave my memory of this peculiar place

MY ORIENTAL SOUL

An ant climbing up
the toilet bowl
slipping all the way

I will give him a raft!

An ant floating on the tissue paper.

ROADFOOD BAKING

The styrofoam pie and
Road food frying in the vats.
Cups of bark
bitter as the miles
that lead you far beyond

    when the newsprint
keeps you warm
    on the parkbench
dept. of parks and humanities

DODGE CITY

Doc Holliday's in town
I saw Bat Masterson!
I heard they run 'em out of Ford County.
Hot work in the town
Bat Masterson's here, Luke Short too!
Charley Bassett and Doc Holliday
holdn' the fort.
Old Tom Moonlight will straighten 'em out.
Luke's sportin' the playful
sunlight beneath his
own vine and fig tree.
He could talk a rattlesnake
into biting itself.

MAJOR GENERAL MOONLIGHT

Knew it was gonna be
    more trouble and less
talk in Dodge City.

When the townsfolk leave their places of business
    they strap their six-shooters on,
a quick eye down the alley
    meets a cat.

The pump turns up sweet water
    and dusty boots
leave an imprint
    on moon soil as we know it.

More trouble in Dodge
    the tension mounted
General Moonlight rode
    down the usual sod trail
of arrowheads sage and Buffalo Bones.

CHANGE

Sometimes people's faces beam with love
sometimes they glow in joy
sometimes a golden haze generates in
the little globe of life.

Many more times than not the
body is dancing and singing
beneath the wounds wanting to
transpose among the bushes
and the exquisite flowers so alone.

Hope does something good for you
it makes you feel warm and plentiful.
The lines in the face are not as sharp
the grip on humanity not as tight
but to let the eyes see full strength
to the feet of great design and meaning.

The feet, those things you walk on
such engineering over millions of years!
Should be bathed and rubbed
while the dust of millions of paths turns to gold,
rolls up into a ball and explodes to
powder the scenery around us.

SUMMER'S ADDITION

A spider,
like a rider
hurries out in the light.

There is nothing around me
but everyday things
and the moon preparing night.

A nudge of subtle wind from winter's broom
inches across a shorter day.

The fireflies are fewer
and the bat swoops lower
the crow struts around like a dude.

Each board I must handle,
each nail too, to make a shape
out of piles of wood.

ON CONTEMPORARY POETRY

                    for Hugh Fox

The dream of shirts has come alive
and marched through morning
like the daddy long legs
who hurries across my map of Mexico
or the lemmings in a line,
down to the sea

How will we save the shirts and
keep them dry and unstained for the future

How can we frame the big window
keep from living in the streets
which are full of snakes
made of electric cords and broken glass
spilling from the junk food palaces

We've labored for change and in our time
can only see it in our clothes

But we can slip into time and
make it long or shorten it
well like a seamstress I suppose

We'll get it said by adjusting space between it
and realigning the fragments we juxtapose

REPORT FROM CHERRY VALLEY

They're still talking about drugs
in the boondocks and small towns
admiring each other's homespun clothing
awaiting the next evangelist

The welfare guitars are booming
to California they've not been
but plan to go there when...

They dot the language with "Whatsisface"
the landscapes remembered by beersigns

I could tell them that I've been there
know how far it is etcetera
but they will say I'm too old
unaware of the ruby Indian
sleeping in their hills

They don't yet know how the dust storm
begins just beneath the skin
and rolls like the change of climate
to our deeper parts and kin

They want to talk to the California bear
and swim in a land we can't go near

$3.00

Cherry Valley Editions
Box 303,
Cherry Valley,
NY 13320